Write your poem here

Poems from a Drawer

By *Ronald Kent*

Cover design by *Ronald Kent*

ISBN: 9780991672721

Createspace ISBN 9781482741339

Createspace ISBN 1482741334

Published By Ronald Kent 2012-09-22

No part of this publication, may be reproduced, stored in, or introduced, into a retrieval system, or transmitted, in any form, or by any means, "electronic, mechanical, photocopying, recording or otherwise," without the prior written permission of the publisher. Any person who does any unauthorized act in relation to this publication may be liable to criminal prosecution and civil claims for damages.

This book is sold to the condition that it shall not, by way of trade or otherwise, be lent, resold, hired out, or otherwise circulated without the publisher's prior consent in any form of binding or cover other than that in which it is published and without a similar condition including this condition being imposed on the subsequent purchaser

Table of Contents

Author Notes

"Scarlett Square was written in response to the red square movement in Montreal. Living through daily protest that cost millions of dollars to save the cost of a cup of coffee, has cost more than the entire group ever fought for. The protesters lost their main goal and most of their support. Taxes in the future will reflect the true cost."

"A "Pig at the Trough" reflects the corruption that seems to be rampant in Montreal and other cities. Governments, Hospitals, City Officials and Earl Jones, what's next?"

"I wrote Seeing Dogs while leaving a counselling session that used a dog to help people cope with stress, after leaving the session; I stopped at a street light while waiting there was a person using a Seeing Eye dog to cross the street, the two connected."

"I wrote this poem, Angles Circle, to reflect the world's sadness and grief form Sandy Hook Elementary. The actions there should say it all, simply tragic."

"Sadly, Anyone's Guess relates too much today, social media like Facebook and other forms create bandwagon type frenzies that destroy people's lives. It seems that we throw a lot of pebbles around; each eventually adds up to a ton. These pebbles are thrown just for a laugh or to gain popularity points by someone. The human mind is fragile and needs compassion to give it strength. The people throwing the pebbles know full well the outcome of their actions; it's the disregard for their actions that's even more disturbing, just pressing send doesn't give you a free pass to demoralize another person."

"It's the Painter, is the first thing I hear. A humorous poem about work, people do leave things hanging around."

"I was simply watching a soccer game and they called it football, in the UK of course, in comparison to football here in Canada. It's an imaginary account of how Football came to be."

"A heavy Christmas morning snow fall in Canada, if you shoveled the stuff, you know what I am talking about."

"I actually wrote this poem twenty years ago in a classroom in Ormstown. It made it into the yearbook."

"This woman is truly wonderful. I could say more but there's not enough space."

"How an individual is treated when young will determine the outcome. Caged in, or free?"

"A chronological account on the effects child abuse has on its victims."

"Dealing with depression and finding meaning, one day I said to myself wouldn't it be great if it could be solved with just an equation that thought spurred the poetry and math combination."

Scarlet Square

This now obtuse shape the scarlet square
Seems too appear, almost everywhere

Meant to symbolize education free
Does have cost, too you and me

They sat too talk the righteous ones
And did leave out, the radical sons

For just one dollar cost per day
Try to make, society pay

Stomp their feet rant and rave
Did not work, we did not cave

Not quite content the students be
Cast a stone, at you and me

Listen now the radical one speak
Meant to incite, the radical weak

Mask themselves the cowards do
As too keep, their anonymity true

Unjust groups can't stand on two
Jump in the other, stomp me and you

Now the group too blind to see
Forced a law, some don't agree

Protest that started something free
Has cost us all, some liberty

The original idea now lost in the air
This scarlet square, I now will beware

By *Ronald Kent*

Pigs at the Trough

Two-witch to another hurly burley's done
Something about battle lost and won
Warrior's today, no need for gun

Pigs at the trough want to drink
Closer look ponder and think
Illusion seen, disorder in-sync

Look to see one's in charge
One's appearance usually quite large
Good with butter, could be marge

Scoffing a meal show of pride
No strait line but side by side
Piglet in waiting holding the ide

Political- banker pig in a suit
Live in the pen of ink repute
Button pressed, firmly on mute

Following rules grandparent's deed
Look to the future seeing the need
Pigs now eager, income is greed

Loose the house everything fails
Rocking more fast biting of nails
Fancy Pigs, sporting coiled tails

Getting older walking with stick
Come to realize it was a trick
Pig in the suit wearing lipstick

Waiting to see if they get caught
Depends on lawyers put in your spot
You need a lawyer one that's not bought

At this age given the screw
Out of money what's one to do
Count on some family to get you through

By Ronald Kent

Seeing Dogs

A seeing dog helps cross the road on green

Just cross the street, wonderful scene

A seeing dog helps when someone sees red

Not losing control, get sad eyes instead

A seeing dog slows getting close to the curb

Seeing it done, really superb

When sullen and sad in depression you lag

A seeing dog nears, with a kiss and a wag.

Holding its harness guides ever so slowly

You'd think powers involved, were sacred and holy

Take comfort to see dog so exceptional

Concerned with the needs, of being accessible

A seeing dog's goal get you home soon

And does it so well, have a nice afternoon

A seeing dog calms ever so slightly

Just calm enough, your thinking more brightly

Seeing dogs see what humans are lacking

Gives to us, unconditional backing

By *Ronald Kent*

Angels Circle

Leader and chief expressing his grief
Sorrow felt heart breaking brief
Opening doors for collective relief

Must be expressed be it hard
Trickle it down reporter in yard
Trouble reading words on a card

Family photos sitting with smile
Tears well up flow like the Nile
Falling on knees praying in aisle

Children not lost but gone before

High up above Angels did soar

Strait to Heaven suffer no more

.

Golden Gates now open wide

Pure precious Children enter inside

Given white wings they easily glide

Are Angels real once they did ask?

In God's love now happy bask

Angels created completing the task

By *Ronald Kent*

Anyone's Guess

Time to change the people that shun
Change the things which have been done
Can things be changed, done by Anyone

Learn from the stone being cast around
Take the time lay stones on the ground
Who's that I see? demanding a pound

Gripping a stone to cast once again
Lots of damage feeling the pain
If I tell you, will you refrain

Probably not so what's one to do
Work on myself see what is true
Please take the time, sit in a pew

Stop asking the question what's wrong with people
They tend to back off, when facing the steeple
Reach out my friend, be like the sepal

Time to ask myself without fear
Find the courage, to seek what is clear
Try not to look at life with a sneer

Know what I see may pretend not to say
Sometimes you have to at the end of the day
We're only human, sometime we stray

Just a defence developed when spun
That's where I think it may have begun
has nothing to do, with you Anyone

By *Ronald Kent*

It's the Painter

I'm just a painter, dressed in white

In your office, painting all night

Never to see me, gone before light

Been told by your boss, you don't like the smell

Here to please you, said what the hell

As long they pay, all will be swell

Now during the night, while moving you desk

Rolled out from under, something grotesque

Left over I'm sure, Christmas burlesque

Next time my dear, watch out for your stock

Guy beside you, he left a sock

Not from Christmas, now I'm in shock

All have nice families, seen in the photos

Girl in the corner, lots of mementos

Guy with the sock though, he drives two Pintos

Painting near done, seen all your shows

Don't feel so bad, that's how it goes

Next time good people, don't leave the clothes

The boss left beside you, a flat folding box

Place all your stuff in, including the clocks

It wasn't just put there, to throw out pet rocks

Well now that I'm done, hope you enjoy

Color you look at, have to be coy

Couldn't tell you, colored blind boy

By *Ronald Kent*

Football to Football

Boys in the UK can play it they say

Huffing and puffing from running all day

One of your players, has gone astray

On the side lines compressing the ball

Enduring the sign of a bad call

Head down in shame, now there's a brawl

Football has points easy to hold

Invent a game say it's not old

Crossing the pond, can it be sold

This isn't rugby ball is too flat

Bumping around no need for that

Pick the ball up, run on a mat

We call it football not really hard

Player to player moving by yard

Judging us not, by using a card

In crowed stands, deep in the thicket

Sits the same lad thinking of cricket

Baseball he ponders, buys him a ticket

By *Ronald Kent*

Some Season's Greeting

You've been sleeping all night and slowly I fell

Inches I dropped in the place where you dwell

Gazing through window you say what the hell

Me, I am winter sometimes bring snow

Awoke you this morning heard my wind blow

Get out the shovel, have work for you Joe

Now don't lift too much here for a while

Neighbors are watching be sure to smile

If you're going to do it, do it in style

Driveway is clean at least for now

From my point of view here comes the plow

More shovelling ahead wipe off that brow

Along with the snow add me some cold

For this my friend you're getting too old

Not so bad if you're digging for gold

Exertion too hard pain in the chest

Is the driveway your final nest?

Off to the doctor have a stress test

Season's for greeting people you love

Don't want to lose you in the snow that you shove

You'll have old man winters view from above

By *Ronald Kent*

Dulce

Time has passed been twenty one years

As time went by, lived through some tears

Can say right now from my point of view

Happy to say, they've been spent with you

During our trek had a small son

Have to say, job that's well done

Watched you mold that boy with finesse

And made sure he left, not looking a mess

Look at our home done up like a castle

Spent quality time there, not without hassle

Made to look easy clipping flowers no fuss

Your gift for sharing, not just for us

Others can see to them it's quite clear

Sometimes I don't, for granted I fear

For those times my love I must confess

I'm truly sorry, you're still my Princess

But that's not all you've now become Queen

Walk with you head up, you must be seen

By *Ronald Kent*

Free Bird

Some birds are caged some birds are free

Who's to say which one you'll be

Depends on the owner who holds the chick's fate

Open up dreams or just shut the gate

Don't clip my wings my chance to fly

Land on your shoulder gaze at the sky

In and out of this cage I will go

Building up confidence trust and ego

Then come a day, out of cage with some shock

Don't be so sad good with the flock

Now keep me caged in what have I learned

Screeching and flapping my anger quite churned

One day escape will come we all know

Head for the door hit the window

No big surprise the owner is glad

Let's get another one that's not mad

By *Ronald Kent*

Hungry Ghost

How was this hungry ghost conceived

From these twelve steps, have perceived

From the womb one to nine

Too much alcohol, drugs and wine

With need to be held caressed and fed

Never to be found, but anger instead

From need to be free was left with he

This deviant person, come sit on my knee

Soon did learn inside my head

Ideas cease to churn, these eyes became dead

From further neglect and tremendous abuse

People soon say, this child is obtuse

The search for love friendship and need

Turns too struggle, it's hard to proceed

Act out and make choices the cost will be high

From this point on, the first row of bricks lie

But do not despair found a way through

With the help of new friends, who said you take some too

This feeling is great give me some more

Not this time friend. It cost to explore

From need to explore whatever the cost

Unable to see, soon become lost

Again people look, they're laughing at me

Enjoying themselves disregarding the fee

Sometimes think, they're blinder then we

We the addicted brain waves dysfunctional

Must dig way down deep to become super punctual

Know this, it's hard, and may seem absurd

Stand up and yell, let yourselves be heard

By Ronald Kent

Class Time

Monday's through Friday's

Weren't always so bliss

Whole lives are changing

Full of what's this

They're trying to teach us

Where listening I'm sure

We keep watching the clock

To head for the door

Classes aren't long

Three hours or so

Five days a week

Then we all go

By *Ronald Kent*

Literary Math Equation

Solving depression

If this equation by Victor Frankl is true

D=S-M

Despair = suffering – meaning

I suffer from despair

My despair causes me suffering

My suffering clouds my true meaning

The clouds stop me from finding my true meaning.

–S+-C=-M

We all need meaning. What is my meaning?

What will my meaning equal to?

When my meaning reaches its equal

What will it mean to me?

How will that meaning change my despair?

What is the meaning in my suffering?

If suffering hurts why not find meaning to stop the suffering

$-M=D+S$

If I obtain meaning I can remove despair and suffering

This equals happiness and then gives me more meaning

$-D-S=H=+M+M+M.........to\ infinity$

Is this equation true?

Author Bio

Ronald kent was born in Newfoundland, Canada. His family had moved to Montreal in the sixties, like all Newfoundlanders who leave the Island, it was in search of work, but still it is said that no Newfoundlander can ever leave. When an Islander dies, no matter where he is, even their souls return home before heading up to the Grand Banks of Heaven. The Author was brought up in three fine districts in the Montreal area, Point St. Charles, Verdun and Little Burgundy.

Ronald purposely writes controversial poems that are meant to spark conversation on subjects most would stay away from. Liking the freedom of being a freelance writer, he has self published six books on subjects such as, sexual abuse, true crime, fictional crime and corruption. He welcomes all reviews positive as well as the negative, both are vital to change.

Titles

Speak Up: deals with the affects sexual abuse has on the abused throughout life, based on true events.

Poems from a Drawer: These poems range from controversial to downright cute.

The future book is a twisted Irish crime novel. This book is fiction and close to being published look for it, it will entertain.

All of these are in eBook form as well as in print.

They can be purchased in print through,

kentronald@hotmail.com

EBooks can be seen on

Google play, Amazon Kindle, Kobo, and Smashwords
sold worldwide.